From the Chef's Kitchen

From the Chef's Kitchen

A collection of recipes from Erickson chefs
throughout the country

From the Chef's Kitchen
Copyright © 2006, Erickson Retirement Communities

First Edition
October 2006
10,000 copies

ISBN 978-0-9789867-0-4
ISBN 0-9789867-0-9

www.Erickson.com

All proceeds from this cookbook will benefit Experience Corps.

Experience Corps offers new adventures in service for Americans over 55. Now in 14 cities, Experience Corps works to solve serious social problems, beginning with literacy. Today more than 1,800 Corps members serve as tutors and mentors to children in urban public schools and after-school programs, where they help teach children to read and to develop the confidence and skills to succeed in school and in life. Research shows that Experience Corps boosts student academic peformance, helps schools and youth-serving organzations become more successful, strengthens ties between these institutions and surrounding neighborhoods, and enhances the well-being of the volunteers in the process. Experience Corps is a signature program of Civic Ventures.

EXPERIENCE
CORPS®
new adventures in service

Acknowledgements

Photography: Joe Fino, Scott Kahn, Vince Lupo, John Makowski, Amy Smith, Bryce Vickmark

Contributing Chefs: Mark Badin, Mohammad Bayan, Scott Brown, David Chiasson, Victor Cirrincione, Ron Colasanti, Mark Diller, Jason Fernandi, Vance Klein, Wayne Knowles, James Little, Jr., Russell Logan, Edward Mandich, Charles Nitsch, Cathie Reichman, James Rondinelli, Terry Shuster, Samuel Soto, Steve Szilvagyi, Jeff Terilli, Marvin Wilson

Chairs: Christy Dennis, Bridget Williams

Design: Matthew Gump, Jolie Kwok, Bridget Williams

Text: Julia Boyle, Wendy Meyeroff, Danielle Rexrode

Public Relations: Kate Newton Schmelyun

Production: Rob Bobbitt, Danielle Bourassa, Zach Cheney, Charlene Curreri, Melissa Cohen, Deborah Dasch, Richard Daub, Wayne Knowles, Alison Marthe, Erin Minnigh, Gale Samborne, Jill Stursa, Jessica Trimble

Table of Contents

Table of Contents

Elegant
Evening

Chefs'
Picks

From the Ch

Introduction

BREAD AND BUTTER ... MILK AND cookies ... some things are just meant to go together.

But let's face it, great food is not the first thing that comes to mind when you think of a retirement community.

It's a widely held stereotype that the food served at retirement communities is about what you'd expect to find at a hospital or high school cafeteria—bland food produced in mass quantities. In fact, most people just concede that they'll have to put their taste buds on the back burner when dining at a retirement community.

To doubting diners everywhere, we say: there are two sides to every story.

Getting It Right

Every day, Erickson communities prove that great cuisine can be prepared on a large scale. And that proof is literally in the pudding. In our case that pudding is Chef Mark Diller's Pear Bread Pudding with Vanilla Sauce (page 24). Mark's pudding is a favorite at Ann's Choice, an Erickson community in Bucks County, Pennsylvania. We've also included popular local dishes like Chef Russell Logan's Maryland Crab Cakes (page 49), new twists on classics like Chef David Chiasson's Pesto Pollo Pizza (page 46), elegant entrées such as Chef Jason Fernandi's Braised Lamb Shank (page 73), and desserts to die for like Chef Steve Szilvagyi's Girl Scout™ Peanut Butter Cream Pie (page 52).

Little Bit of Everything

We've included more than fifty sumptuous recipes in *From the Chef's Kitchen*. "From The Menu" features our favorite foods from our different restaurant menus. These are the dishes that became part of our menu thanks to people

ef's Kitchen

requesting them time and time again. "Pub & Bistro" is a collection of quick and simple appetizers, soups, salads, and sandwiches from our on-site pub and café menus. These casual, yet creative recipes are great for lunch and the perfect light fare. Our "Elegant Evening" recipes capture some of our most popular daily "specials" where decadence rules the day. And like your grandma's famous sour cherry pie recipe, "Chefs' Picks" are the recipes that we love— favorite dishes that have been passed down from our families and friends throughout the years.

Many of these dishes are quite easy to make and you'll find you probably have all of the ingredients already in your kitchen. Other recipes are a bit more complicated, but we're confident even the casual cook can pull them off. They've been tested by our families, friends, and many have been prepared at our own communities. And since most of you aren't trying to feed an army,

we've adjusted our recipes to yield more average servings.

Recipe for Success

So what has twenty-three years of cooking for upwards of 18,000 people in nine states and growing taught us?

For one thing, quality never has to suffer just because your quantity increases. Whether you're cooking an intimate dinner for two or catering a celebration for two hundred, the same rules apply: good recipes + fresh ingredients = great food.

Food is a symbol of love and family. When it comes to good food, at Erickson our philosophy is simple: make it just like Mom used to make. We pour our hearts and souls into every dish we make and we hope that you'll enjoy sharing these recipes with your family for years to come. ★

From the Menu

You know your favorite food? The one you can eat again and again without ever tiring of it. It could be your grandmother's pot roast or maybe it's your aunt's homemade mile high apple pie. "From the Menu" features the foods we all love to eat. They're classic recipes you've enjoyed a hundred times and still want to eat a hundred more. Think of these luscious hearty recipes for your next Sunday supper, pot luck dish, or weeknight dinner with plenty of leftovers for the next day's lunch. ☆

"When cooking, keep it simple. People like to recognize what they're eating, not have to guess what's on their plate."

-Russell Logan, Oak Crest

"Food is not about impressing people. It's about making them feel comfortable."

-Ina Garten, *The Barefoot Contessa*

Bermuda Fish Chowder

Serves 4

$3^1/_2$ teaspoons olive oil
$1^3/_4$ teaspoons garlic, minced
$2^1/_2$ tablespoons carrot, diced
$^1/_4$ cup onion, diced
$2^1/_2$ tablespoons celery, diced
$2^1/_2$ tablespoons leeks, diced
$2^1/_3$ tablespoons green pepper, diced
$3^1/_2$ tablespoons potato, diced
$1^1/_4$ cups tomato, diced
$2^1/_4$ cups clam juice
$^1/_8$ teaspoon hot sauce
$^1/_8$ teaspoon bay leaf, ground
$3^1/_2$ teaspoons fresh parsley, chopped
3 teaspoons cornstarch
$2^1/_3$ tablespoons water
$2^1/_4$ ounces cod loin, diced

Sauté garlic, carrot, onion, leeks, celery, and green pepper in olive oil until they are soft, but do not brown. Add potato; allow to cook until tender. Add tomatoes, clam juice, bay leaf, hot sauce, and parsley.

Bring mixture to a slow simmer. Combine cornstarch and water in a small bowl and stir to a thin paste. Stir slowly into chowder.

Continue cooking at a slow simmer for 50 minutes. Add cod. Cook 10 to 15 minutes or until fish is thoroughly cooked.

Maryland Crab Soup

Serves 12

2 whole steamed crabs, fresh or frozen
8 cups water
$\frac{1}{2}$ cup frozen mixed vegetables
$\frac{1}{4}$ pound potatoes, peeled and diced
1 tablespoon Old Bay™ seasoning or crab boil
1$\frac{1}{2}$ tablespoons fish or chicken bouillon
1 cup canned tomatoes, diced
$\frac{1}{4}$ pound crab claw or backfin crabmeat
Old Bay™ seasoning to taste

Remove and discard top shell of crabs. Add whole crabs to water and boil. Cook for one hour. Strain liquid. Crack and reserve meat from claws to put back in soup. Add remaining ingredients, including the claw meat, and simmer for one hour.

Old Bay™ is a regional seasoning and may be hard to find outside of Maryland. In spice grinder combine 1 tablespoon celery salt, 2 teaspoons salt, 3 bay leaves, $\frac{3}{4}$ teaspoon brown mustard seeds, $\frac{1}{2}$ teaspoon black peppercorns, 10 allspice berries, 10 cloves, $\frac{1}{2}$ teaspoon paprika, $\frac{1}{8}$ teaspoon cayenne pepper, $\frac{1}{8}$ teaspoon ground ginger, $\frac{1}{8}$ teaspoon ground mace, $\frac{1}{8}$ teaspoon cardamom (removed from pods), and a pinch of ground cinnamon. Grind to a coarse powder (makes about 2 tablespoons).

Rosemary Roasted Sweet Potato Wedges

Serves 3

3 medium sweet potatoes
2 tablespoons unsalted butter, melted
1 teaspoon fresh rosemary leaves
Salt and pepper to taste

Preheat oven to 400°.

Cut potatoes lengthwise into $\frac{1}{2}$-inch slices. In large mixing bowl, toss potatoes with butter and rosemary. Salt and pepper to taste.

Transfer potatoes to roasting pan or baking sheet. Cook 10 minutes, then turn. Cook additional 10 minutes or until tender.

Honey and Ginger Glazed Carrots

Serves 4

$\frac{3}{4}$ pound carrots, peeled
$2\frac{1}{4}$ teaspoons honey
$1\frac{1}{2}$ teaspoons unsalted butter
$\frac{3}{4}$ teaspoon fresh gingerroot, peeled and finely diced

Cut carrots in half length wise, then cut into 1-inch wedges.

In a stockpot, cover carrots with salted water by about 2 inches. Boil uncovered about 10 minutes or until tender.

While carrots cook, combine honey, butter, and ginger in small saucepan and cook over moderate heat until butter melts. Transfer mixture to large mixing bowl.

Drain carrots well and toss with honey glaze. Season with salt and pepper to taste.

David Chiasson
Executive Chef, Brooksby
Peabody, Massachusetts

Formal training and experience: As a young man, David had the good fortune of training with a French chef from the ages of 14 to 18 and then attended Newbury College in Brookline, Massachusetts. He also traveled to France on a Food and Wine Culinary tour and worked the Anthony Spinnazola Gala at the World Trade Center in Boston.

"I attribute my passion for food as the secret to being a good chef. French and Italian cuisine are my favorites, and the one rule that I live by is to use the freshest ingredients possible. Fresh herbs are always a nice touch to any dish."

Out of the kitchen: "I enjoy traveling and working in my garden. I'm also an equestrian and have been riding horses for over 20 years." ☆

" Fresh herbs

are a nice

touch

to any

dish. **"**

David Chiasson

Buttermilk Chicken

Serves 4

4 boneless, skinless chicken breasts (approximately 1 pound)
2 cups buttermilk
2 cups all-purpose flour
1 cup breadcrumbs
½ teaspoon lemon pepper
½ teaspoon tarragon
½ teaspoon paprika
½ cup melted margarine
Salt and pepper to taste
1 cup mustard salad dressing
1 teaspoon chopped chives

Marinate chicken in buttermilk in covered, non-metallic container and refrigerate.

Discard marinade and combine dry ingredients in mixing bowl.

Dredge chicken into the flour mixture, coating well.

Place chicken on greased baking pan.

Drizzle margarine over chicken being careful not to drench the chicken.

Bake at 375° for approximately 40 to 45 minutes or until internal temperature reaches 165°.

Drizzle chicken with mustard dressing. Top with chives and serve immediately.

{ chef profile }

> " I always pay attention to **details** because presentation is **everything**. "

Jeff Terrilli
Chef de Cuisine, Brooksby
Peabody, Massachusetts

Formal training and experience: Jeff was born into the food industry as his parents and grandparents owned a small food and deli shop. He attended Newbury College in Brookline, Massachusetts, where he earned an Outstanding Achievement Award in the Field of Ice Carving. His experience in the kitchen includes Simply Elegant Catering, Legal Seafoods, and Bertucci's.

"I love the theme nights we create here at Brooksby. I enjoy being able to cook with recipes from all over the world. I always look for little touches or 'extras' I can do to elevate the dining experience. 'You eat with your eyes' is a famous expression, so I always pay attention to details because presentation is everything."

Out of the kitchen: "I live for two things in life: food and football. I am an avid autograph collector. I have autographs from sports figures and actors like Bruce Lee, Marilyn Monroe, and Tom Hanks. And I love wrestling." ☆

Breaded Chicken Medallions and Dijon Chive Cream Sauce

Serves 3

3 boneless, skinless chicken breasts,
   cut into 2-inch pieces
4 eggs, beaten
$\frac{1}{4}$ cup water
$\frac{1}{2}$ cup flour
1 cup Italian-style breadcrumbs
1 cup olive oil, divided
1 tablespoon garlic, freshly chopped
$\frac{1}{2}$ cup white wine (chablis or chardonnay)
3 tablespoons dijon mustard
3 tablespoons fresh chives, finely chopped
3 cups half-and-half
1 teaspoon salt
1 teaspoon pepper
1 tablespoon cornstarch
1 tablespoon water
6 ounces uncooked rigatoni
   or penne pasta
$\frac{1}{4}$ cup fresh chives, chopped (for garnish)

Cook pasta al dente. Drain and set aside. Dredge chicken in flour, shaking off excess. In separate bowl, combine eggs and water. Dip chicken into egg mixture, coating well. Dredge chicken in breadcrumbs, coating well.

Heat $\frac{1}{2}$ cup olive oil in sauté pan. Add chicken, reduce heat to medium-low, and sauté until chicken is browned on both sides and cooked completely.

Transfer chicken to platter and keep warm. Discard oil from sauté pan, wiping pan clean. Heat remaining $\frac{1}{2}$ cup olive oil and sauté garlic until tender, making sure not to brown. Add white wine and cook until wine reduces by half.

Whisk in mustard, chives, salt, and pepper. Add half-and-half. In small bowl, mix together cornstarch and water; add to mustard sauce. Allow sauce to thicken; return chicken to pan and add pasta.

Toss chicken and pasta with sauce. Garnish with chives and serve.

Beef Pot Roast with Vegetables

Serves 4

1½ pounds beef round inside top
⅛ teaspoon black pepper
¼ teaspoon granulated garlic
1 teaspoon beef base
¾ cup water
1 cup tomato, diced
1 medium carrot, diced
1 small yellow onion, diced
1 small Spanish onion, diced
2 ribs celery, diced
1 medium potato, diced
2½ teaspoons margarine
2½ teaspoons all-purpose flour

Preheat oven to 400°.

Season beef with pepper and garlic. Place in roasting pan and cook for 20 minutes.

Reduce temperature to 300°.

Combine beef base and water and add to roasting pan. Do not pour over roast. Cover pan with foil, sealing edges carefully. Continue to braise in oven for additional 45 minutes or until internal temperature reaches about 150° to 155°.

Remove roast from oven and add vegetables. Cover and continue to cook until roast's internal temperature has reached 170° and vegetables are almost tender (add more water during cooking if needed).

Combine flour and margarine in saucepan over low heat, stirring lightly to make a roux. Remove meat and vegetables from gravy and set aside.

Add roux to roasting pan and thicken gravy. Return vegetables to roasting pan. When meat has slightly cooled, slice and serve immediately with vegetables and gravy.

Ham Steak with Cider Raisin Sauce

Serves 2

1 small onion, finely chopped
1½ cups apple cider
2 tablespoon cider vinegar
1 teaspoon mustard seed
1 teaspoon dijon mustard
1 tablepoon olive oil
2 ham steaks ½-inch thick
1 teaspoon fresh gingerroot, peeled and grated
2 tablespoons unsalted butter
¼ cup raisins
1 tablespoon freshly chopped parsley

Mix cider, vinegar, mustard, and mustard seed together in non-metallic bowl and set aside.

In heavy skillet heat olive oil over moderately high heat. Sauté ham steaks about 4 minutes on each side. Transfer to warm plates and keep warm.

Pour off grease from sauté pan and add onion and gingerroot. Cook for about 1 minute. Add cider mixture, stirring occasionally, until reduced by half (about 5 minutes). Add raisins to sauce and whisk in butter and parsley.

Pour sauce over ham and serve warm.

Braised Beef

Serves 8

3 pounds top butt sirloin, cut into
$\frac{1}{2}$-inch thick steaks
2 tablespoons vegetable oil
2 teaspoons salt, divided
2 teaspoons black pepper, divided
1 cup all-purpose flour
1 teaspoon thyme
2 bay leaves
3 cloves fresh garlic, minced
1 orange, juiced and zested
12 ounces beer (dark preferred)
$\frac{2}{3}$ cup beef base (or broth)
6 tablespoons tomato paste
4 cups water
1 onion, rough cut
1 carrot, rough cut

Garnish:
20 pearl onions
1 cup mini carrots
3 ribs celery, diced large
1 bunch parsley, finely chopped

Optional Vegetables:
1 cup Brussels sprouts, halved and par boiled
1 cup turnips, diced and par boiled
1 cup rutabagas, peeled, diced, and par boiled

Heat large braising pan on stove. Preheat oven to 320°. Dust meat with flour and half of salt and pepper. Add oil to pan and heat. Brown beef, a few pieces at a time, on high heat. Remove from pan when brown on all sides.

Add onion and carrot. Reduce heat to low. Add garlic and thyme and allow to slow cook until onion is soft.

Add beer, beef base, garnish ingredients, and water. Bring to a boil, add orange juice, orange zest, bay leaves, and tomato paste. While still boiling, add beef. Bring back to a boil and remove from heat. Cover and cook in pre-heated oven for one hour.

After 1 hour, check beef for tenderness. Also taste liquid and season with salt and pepper as needed. Return to oven if meat is not cooked to desiered tenderness.

Using tongs, remove meat from liquid and set aside. Strain liquid and bring to boil on stove. Taste and adjust seasonings. Thicken liquid with a cornstarch and water solution to a sauce-like consistency.

Add beef back to pot and stir in parsley. If using optional vegetables, add now. Garnish and serve with mashed potatoes and crusty sour dough bread.

Chicken Pot Pie

Serves 6

2$\frac{1}{2}$ tablespoons margarine
2$\frac{1}{2}$ tablespoons all-purpose flour
2$\frac{1}{8}$ teaspoons chicken base
$\frac{3}{4}$ cup hot water
$\frac{1}{4}$ cup carrot, diced
3 tablespoons potato, diced
2$\frac{1}{2}$ tablespoons onion, diced
3$\frac{1}{2}$ tablespoons celery, diced
2 cups white meat chicken,
   diced, cooked
2$\frac{1}{2}$ tablespoons frozen green pea
6 (6$\frac{3}{4}$-inch) pie pastry crusts
1$\frac{1}{8}$ teaspoons water
1 egg

Preheat oven to 425°.

Heat margarine. Add flour gradually. Stir with whisk and cook 10 minutes to make a roux.

Combine chicken base and hot water; stir to dissolve thoroughly. Gradually add to roux; stir until smooth. Bring to a simmer, stirring often. Cook carrot, potato, onion, and celery in steamer or boiling water until tender. Drain well.

Add vegetables to roux mixture; carefully stir in chicken and peas. Divide mixture evenly among 6 small round gratin dishes. Cover each with a pastry crust.

Combine egg and water to make an egg wash. Brush top of crust with egg wash. Bake for 25 to 30 minutes until hot and crust is golden brown.

Chef tip: Substitute one egg with two egg whites for a fat and cholesterol free alternative.

23

Pear Bread Pudding and Vanilla Sauce

Serves 6

Pudding

4 eggs, beaten
¾ cup sugar
3 cups milk
1 tablespoon vanilla extract
8 slices egg bread, crusts removed
4 tablespoons butter, softened
1 (16-ounce) can sliced pears, drained

Preheat oven to 350°.

Grease 9 x 9 inch baking dish.

Combine eggs and sugar in large bowl. Gradually stir in milk and vanilla; set aside.

Lightly spread both sides of bread with butter. Arrange layer of bread slices in dish; top with another layer of bread slices. Arrange pear slices on bread. Pour egg mixture over bread and pears; let stand 30 minutes.

Bake 45 minutes or until mixture is puffed and a knife inserted in the center comes out clean.

Vanilla Sauce

½ cup sugar
1½ tablespoons all-purpose flour
1½ tablespoons cornstarch
2¼ cups milk
2 egg yolks, beaten
1 tablespoon butter
2 teaspoons vanilla extract

Combine sugar, flour, and cornstarch in large saucepan.

Gradually whisk in milk. Cook over medium heat, stirring constantly, until mixture comes to a boil, 3 to 5 minutes. Remove from heat.

Stir 1 cup hot mixture into egg yolks. Stir egg yolk mixture back into hot mixture; return to heat, stirring constantly, until mixture is bubbly.

Remove from heat, stir in butter and vanilla extract.

To serve, ladle vanilla sauce on dessert plate and top with warm bread pudding.

Strawberry Shortcake

Serves 5

$^1/_2$ cup + 1 tablespoon all-purpose flour
$2^1/_4$ teaspoons baking powder
5 teaspoons solid shortening
$^1/_4$ cup + 5 teaspoons milk
$1^3/_4$ teaspoons sugar
$^3/_8$ teaspoon salt
1 small egg, beaten
$2^1/_2$ cups sliced strawberries
Whipped topping for garnish

Preheat oven to 450°.

Combine flour and baking powder. Cut shortening into flour until crumbly.

Combine milk, sugar, salt, and egg. Mix well and add to flour mixture. Mix lightly.

Pat out dough on floured board to 1-inch thickness. Fold all four corners into center. Repeat folding 2 or 3 more times.

Roll out dough to 1-inch thickness. Cut with a 2-inch cutter and place on ungreased baking sheet. Bake for 12 to 15 minutes.

Split biscuits in half. Place bottom half in sherbet dish and spoon $^1/_4$ cup strawberries over top. Place top of biscuit on strawberries. Ladle another $^1/_4$ cup strawberries over top. Top each shortcake with a dollop of whipped topping. Serve immediately.

Special Apple Pie

Makes one 10-inch pie

Crust:
1¾ cups all-purpose flour
¼ cup sugar
1 teaspoon cinnamon
½ teaspoon salt
1¼ sticks butter
¼ cup water or apple cider

Filling:
8 Macintosh apples, peeled, cored, and sliced
1⅔ cups sour cream
1 cup sugar
⅓ cup all-purpose flour
1 egg, well beaten
2 teaspoons vanilla
½ teaspoon salt

Topping:
1 cup chopped walnuts or pecans
½ cup all-purpose flour
⅓ cup firmly packed brown sugar
⅓ cup granulated sugar
1 tablespoon cinnamon
Pinch of salt
1 stick butter, room temperature

For crust:

Combine flour, sugar, cinnamon, and salt in medium bowl. Cut in butter using a pastry blender or 2 knives, until mixture resembles coarse meal. Add water or apple cider and toss mixture gently with fork until evenly moistened. Shape gently into ball.

Transfer to lightly floured board and roll into circle slightly larger than a 10-inch deep-dish pie plate. Ease pastry into plate and flute edge. Set aside.

For filling:

Preheat oven to 450°.

Combine all ingredients in a large bowl and mix well. Spoon into crust and bake for 10 minutes.

Reduce oven temperature to 350° and continue baking until filling is slightly puffed and golden brown, about 40 minutes. (If edges of crust begin to brown too quickly, cover with strips of aluminum foil.)

For topping:

Meanwhile, combine walnuts, flour, sugars, cinnamon, and salt in medium bowl and mix well. Blend in butter until mixture is crumbly. Spoon over pie and bake 15 minutes longer.

Spiced Applesauce Cake

Serves 12

½ cup chopped walnuts
½ cup unsalted butter, room
   temperature
1 cup granulated sugar
1 cup unsweetened applesauce
1 egg, beaten
1½ cups all-purpose flour
4 teaspoons baking powder
1 teaspoon ground cinnamon
½ teaspoon salt
½ teaspoon ground nutmeg
¼ teaspoon ground cloves
¼ teaspoon ground allspice

Optional brown-butter icing:
½ cup unsalted butter
3 cups confectioners' sugar
2 teaspoons vanilla extract
1 tablespoon heavy cream

Preheat oven to 375°. Butter and flour 9 x 5 x 3-inch loaf pan and tap out excess flour.

Spread the walnuts on a baking sheet and toast in oven until they begin to color and are fragrant, 5 to 7 minutes. Remove from oven and transfer to a small bowl to cool.

In a large bowl, beat together butter and granulated sugar until light and fluffy. Add applesauce and egg and mix well.

In a bowl, sift together flour, baking powder, cinnamon, salt, nutmeg, cloves, and allspice. Add ¼ cup of flour mixture to walnuts and stir to coat. Add remaining flour mixture to applesauce mixture and stir until thoroughly combined.

Fold in walnuts, and pour into the prepared pan. Bake until a toothpick inserted into center comes out clean, about 1 hour and 10 minutes.

Meanwhile, make icing, if desired. In a small saucepan over medium-high heat, melt butter and continue to cook until it is the color of a brown paper bag, about 4 minutes. Remove from heat and beat in confectioners' sugar until smooth. Add vanilla and enough cream to form a spreadable mixture.

Transfer cake to a rack and let cool in the pan for 10 to 15 minutes. If serving cake plain, turn out onto the rack and let it cool completely.

If serving cake with icing, set warm cake on a rack over a plate or pan. Pour icing over the top, letting it drip down the sides. Let stand until set, 20 to 25 minutes. Cut into slices and serve.

Pub & Bistro

Some of the best food can be found in the most unexpected of places. Have you ever wandered into a neighborhood pub or a local café to indulge in their famed hot corned beef sandwich or a steaming crock of French onion soup?

Quite often some of the best homemade desserts are artfully displayed in glass-enclosed counters tempting you to take a taste. From delectable sweets and fragrant soups to fresh salads and mouthwatering sandwiches, these recipes are meant to be prepared with love and enjoyed with friends. They're deliciously simple, yet complex in taste. ★

"Cooking is a balancing act, especially when you have guests with different dietary needs. If you take out the salt for one, the sugar for another, and the fat for another, you have no flavor. So serve a variety of foods—that way everyone has something they can enjoy!"

-Mark Badin, Charlestown

"Working in a restaurant at a young age, I enjoyed the instant gratification of seeing people enjoy my creations."

-Ron Colasanti, Henry Ford Village

Baked Brie Wheel with Walnut Crust and Apple Cider Sauce

Serves 6

Brie
1 brie wheel
**1 cup walnut crumb
    mixture (¾ chopped
    walnuts, ¼ bread
    crumbs)**
**Egg wash (mix 1 egg with
    1⅛ teaspoon water)**
Vegetable oil for frying

Dip brie in egg wash, then coat well with walnut crumb mixture. Deep fry brie until golden brown or sauté in a non-stick skillet.

Place in 350° oven for 3 minutes.

Garnish
2 orange slices
1 kiwi slice
2 strawberries
8 grapes
**2 ounces strawberry
    sauce**

Pool strawberry sauce in 10-inch plate and place brie over it.

Surround with fruit.

Apple Cider Sauce
1 quart apple cider
2 shallots, minced
¼ cup cider vinegar
2 dashes hot sauce
Cinnamon stick
½ tablespoon cornstarch

In a medium saucepan, combine all ingredients except cornstarch. Bring to a boil then lower heat and cook until somewhat reduced.

Remove cinnamon stick and discard. Meanwhile, stir cornstarch into small amount of cold water to make a thin paste. Whisk into hot cider reduction and stir to desired thickness.

Spoon warm sauce over brie before serving.

Terry Shuster
Chef de Cuisine, Fox Run
Novi, Michigan

Formal training and experience: Inspired by the chefs at the restaurant where he worked as a dishwasher, Terry began his culinary arts training at Schoolcraft College and City College of San Francisco. He went on to become the executive chef at the Fox and Hounds Restaurant in Bloomfield, Michigan, for 16 years.

"I believe that any success I enjoy can be attributed to keeping it simple, while at the same time, looking ahead. My rule of thumb is: never create a monster of a menu that cannot be executed properly. You can raise the bar high but keep it achievable."

Out of the kitchen: "I enjoy gardening, golfing, and I'm currently rehabbing an old house." ✫

" Any success I enjoy can be attributed to keeping it simple. "

Gazpacho

Serves 10

2 (46-ounce) cans tomato juice
2 cups water
1 cucumber, peeled, seeded, and finely diced
1 tablespoon fresh garlic, minced
¼ cup red bell pepper, cubed
¼ cup green pepper, cubed
¼ cup Spanish onion, cubed
¼ cup zucchini, cubed
¼ cup carrots, cubed
1 tablespoon sugar
3 tablespoons red wine vinegar
1 tablespoon olive oil
½ teaspoon cayenne pepper
dash of hot sauce
1 tablespoon chives, chopped
2 tablespoons cilantro, chopped
2 tablespoons scallions, chopped
Salt and pepper to taste

Mix together tomato juice, water, diced cucumber, and minced garlic in a large bowl.

Place red and green peppers, Spanish onion, zucchini, and carrot in food processor–pulse twice then add to tomato mixture.

Add remaining ingredients, stir, and chill well before serving.

French Onion Soup

Serves 6

1½ cups Spanish onion, julienned
2 tablespoons butter or butter alternative
1 tablespoon beef base
1½ teaspoons chicken base (no MSG)
1 quart water
4 tablespoons burgundy cooking wine
⅛ teaspoon thyme leaves
Black pepper to taste
3 cups croutons
1 cup shredded swiss cheese

Sauté onion and butter in a large saucepan until well carmelized. Add water, wine, base, and seasonings and bring to a boil. Simmer uncovered for one hour.

To serve, ladle soup into ovenproof bowls and top with croutons and cheese. If desired, place soup bowls on a baking sheet and broil briefly to melt cheese.

Ron Colasanti
Executive Chef, Henry Ford Village
Dearborn, Michigan

Formal training and experience: Beginning as a bus boy at the age of 15, Ron worked his way to salad maker, sauté cook, and then grill cook before receiving his formal training at the Culinary Institute of America, New York. He was chef at Dayton Hudson's Market Place Restaurant and opened Mystic Gourmet and Clever Cooks, a forty-seat, upscale deli, café, and catering company.

"When I was a young boy I would come home from school and there would always be something cooking: pasta sauces, soup, lasagna, or bread baking. I loved the smell of all that food cooking. My mom and grandmother were definitely the two greatest influences in inspiring my cooking career. Working in a restaurant at a young age, I enjoyed the instant gratification of seeing people enjoy my creations. Henry Ford Village has given me the opportunity to interact on a nightly basis with patrons."

Out of the kitchen: "I enjoy spending time with my wife and baby girl. I am a die-hard Detroit Lions fan and season ticket holder. I hope to attend every major sports event at some point in my life." ✫

"I would come home from school and there would always be something cooking."

Chicken Pastina Soup

Serves 12

Stock:
2 gallons chicken broth or stock
**3 pounds stock vegetables: rough
cut carrots, parsnip, celery,
onion, or any other vegetables
on hand**

Soup:
4 medium onions, diced small
**1 bunch celery, sliced or small
diced**
1½ pounds carrots, sliced
¼ to ½ cup olive oil
3 tablespoons olive oil
3 tablespoons butter
8 garlic cloves, minced
8 garlic cloves, chopped
**7 pounds chicken (whole bird or
bone-in legs, thighs, or breasts)**
**1 head Escarole lettuce, trimmed,
washed, and chopped**
**Cooked pastina (allow 1 cup per
serving of soup)**
4 tablespoons dried basil

3 teaspoons dried thyme
Fresh parsley, chopped for garnish
Parmesan cheese for garnish
Salt and white pepper to taste

In a large stock pot add butter and stock vegetables; sauté vegetables for five minutes. Add broth or stock and bring to a simmer.

In a large sauté pan add olive oil and let pan warm. When hot, add chicken and chopped garlic. Sauté chicken until golden brown, then add chicken to stock pot. Simmer chicken stock for about two hours, skimming surface as needed.

In a large sauté pan add the 3 tablespoons olive oil and let pan warm. When hot, add minced garlic, sliced carrots, celery, and diced onions. Sauté about 3 to 5 minutes. Add basil, thyme, salt, and pepper to taste. Cook another 5 minutes, adding a ladle of stock if pan becomes too dry. Set aside.

Remove chicken from stock pot and let cool. Pull off skin and remove meat from bones. Pull or shred chicken into bite size pieces. Set aside.

Strain stock to remove stock vegetables and discard them. Return stock to pot. Add the sautéed seasoned vegetables, shredded chicken, and Escarole to stock pot. Bring to a simmer. Cook about 10 minutes.

Taste. Adjust seasoning with salt, pepper, basil, or thyme as needed.

To serve, spoon about 1 cup of pasta into each soup bowl. Ladle chicken soup over pastina, garnish with fresh parsley and Parmesan cheese.

Chef tip: Refrigerated leftover soup will keep for 3 days. You can also freeze the leftover soup.

{ chef profile }

Joseph Marinelli
Executive Chef, Seabrook
Tinton Falls, New Jersey

Formal training and experience: Having worked in restaurants since age 12, Joseph went on to receive formal training at Johnson & Wales University College of Culinary Arts. He most recently enjoyed working as a gourmet Italian chef at the Trump Plaza in Atlantic City and at Flick International.

"After years of working in the food industry, I consider Seabrook to be the best job yet. I love the energy that's here—the dedication of the staff and the people who live here is tremendous! I believe it takes dedication, a willingness to learn, and using the freshest ingredients to become a good chef."

Out of the kitchen: "I enjoy spending time with Baxter, my German Shepherd, and practicing Muay Thai kickboxing." ☆

> " Dedication, a willingness to learn, and using **fresh** foods are what, I believe, make a **good** chef. "

Tuscan Salad

Serves 1

3 tomatoes, chopped
1 yellow pepper, chopped
1 red onion, julienned
1 bunch arugula, chopped
½ cup olives, sliced
2 teaspoons garlic, chopped
1 (½-inch thick) slice
   panzanella bread
1 cup olive oil
1 red pepper, chopped
1 cucumber, skinned, seeded,
   and diced
1 yellow tomato, chopped
½ cup basil, chopped
1 teaspoon capers
1 eggplant
2 parsnip strips
Leeks strips for garnish
½ cup balsamic vinegar

Make the salad

Toss tomato, cucumber, pepper, onion, arugula, olives, capers, garlic, and basil with olive oil and balsamic vinegar.

Make eggplant ring

Preheat oven to 450°.

Slice eggplant to ½-inch thickness; cut out center. Place slices on a lightly greased baking pan and brush tops with olive oil.

Cook for 5 minutes.

Make crouton

Cut a 5-inch diameter circle from center of panzanella bread slice.

Rub with oil, sprinkle with salt and pepper, and roast in 450° oven until lightly browned.

Place crouton in center of entrée plate, top with eggplant ring and fill with Tuscan salad.

Fry leeks and parsnips. Stand strips of parsnips in the back of salad and top with fried leeks.

39

Cucumber Salad

Serves 4

2 cucumbers, peeled and
   thinly sliced
Salt to taste
$^1/_2$ **yellow onion, finely minced**
$^1/_2$ **cup red wine vinegar**
$^1/_2$ **cup water**
2 teaspoons sugar
$^1/_8$ **teaspoon sweet paprika**
Pinch of dill
**1 small tomato, seeded and
finely chopped (optional)**

Place sliced cucumbers in
a bowl and lightly toss with
salt. Allow to rest for 30
minutes.

Drain cucumbers and lightly press to rid excess water.
They should be slightly limp
but still crisp.

Mix remaining ingredients
together and pour mixture over
cucumbers. Add tomato, if
using, and toss lightly. Marinate
in refrigerator for 1$^1/_2$ hours
before serving.

Tuna Stuffed Tomato

Serves 4

2 (6-ounce cans) albacore tuna, packed
    in water
¼ cup celery, chopped fine
2 tablespoons scallions and chives,
    chopped fine
1 teaspoon lemon juice
1 dash black pepper
¼ cup dill pickle, minced
3 tablespoons mayonnaise
4 (3-ounce) tomatoes

Garnish:
leaf lettuce
cucumber slices
carrot sticks
wheat crackers

Drain tuna and place in stainless mixing bow; break apart with a fork. Add all other ingredients and mix until well blended. Chill immediately.

Remove core from tomato. Cut tomato almost through into eight equal wedges.

Spread tomato wedges apart, creating room to insert tuna salad. Place a scoop of tuna salad into the tomato.

Place tomato on plate that has been lined with leaf lettuce. Garnish with cucumber slices, carrot sticks, and wheat crackers.

Repeat for each tomato used.

Chef tip: Try 1½ tablespoons of reduced-fat mayonnaise plus 1½ tablespoons of low-fat yogurt for a healthy alternative to regular mayonnaise.

{ chef profile }

> **"** I think **honesty**
>
> is the most
>
> important **quality**
>
> a **good** chef
>
> can have. **"**

Victor Cirrincione
Executive Chef, Riderwood
Silver Spring, Maryland

Formal training and experience: After training at Adirondack Community College, Victor enjoyed a successful career at many popular dining venues, including the Sagamore Resort in New York, the Equinox Hotel in Vermont, the Boar's Head Inn, the Kingsmill Resort, and the Inn at Little Washington—a 5-Star, 5-Diamond Inn in Virginia.

"I think honesty is the most important quality a good chef can have—a chef who can stand by his product, good or bad, admit to his faults, be humble with his successes, and recognize those who helped make him successful. At Riderwood I enjoy the interaction I have every day with the people I serve. They're really a joy to be around."

Out of the kitchen: "I truly enjoy going on long drives in the country, going to little towns and trying the local food, and seeing the sights. When I can, I love to fish on the Chesapeake Bay." ☆

The Power Wrap

Serves 1

4 ounces medium rare roast beef, sliced thin
¼ cup smoked Gouda cheese, grated
3 slices tomato
1 large lettuce leaf, shredded
3 tablespoons mayonnaise
½ teaspoon horseradish
1 (10-inch) spinach-flavored flour tortilla

Place tortilla on cutting surface. Mix horseradish with mayonnaise; spread mixture evenly over the half of the tortilla nearest you, stopping about ½-inch from the edge. Sprinkle cheese over mayonnaise.

Top with roast beef, tomato, and lettuce; taking the end closest to you, fold the edge about 1 inch over the filling and roll half way. Then fold in the sides to the right and left in toward the center— make nice and tight. Continue to roll, when completed— the wrap should look like a giant egg roll.

Cut wrap in half serve with fresh fruit and chips.

Grilled Breast of Chicken Sandwich

Serves 1

Herb Mayonnaise:
$\frac{1}{4}$ **teaspoon dill**
$\frac{1}{4}$ **teaspoon tarragon**
$\frac{1}{2}$ **cup mayonnaise**

Sandwich:
1 (4-ounce) grilled boneless, skinless chicken breast
1 whole wheat kosher roll, toasted
1 leaf of lettuce
2 slices tomato
3 tablespoons Herb Mayonnaise
1 slice cheese, optional

Mix all of the Herb Mayonnaise ingredients together.

Spread mayonnaise evenly on both sides of the toasted kosher roll.

Place chicken on bottom half of kosher roll and top with cheese (if desired), lettuce, and tomato and gently place top half of bun on top.

Chef tip: Try fat-free Italian dressing in place of the Herb Mayonnaise, or make the mayonnaise using $\frac{1}{4}$ cup yogurt and $\frac{1}{4}$ cup mayonnaise.

Corned Beef Sandwich

Serves 4

8 slices marble rye
12 ounces corned beef, thin shaved
2 kosher pickle spears
2 tablespoons dijon mustard
4 slices cheese

Pile shaved corned beef and cheese onto a slice of bread. The meat must be stacked high and placed in the center of slice of bread. Top with second slice of bread; cut sandwich in half diagonally. When cutting sandwich use a bread knife and don't press down. Use the knife as you would a saw, back and forth using little downward pressure. Garnish the plate with a kosher dill pickle spear and serve with a ramekin of dijon mustard.

Chef tip: Cooked corned beef must be chilled well prior to slicing. Shaving cooked beef is an art. Slicing meats won't produce the same results as shaving. Shaving produces an extremely thin product that will appear to have more volume, may be piled high, and will be much more tender and moist to the taste.

Pesto Pollo Pizza

Pizza Crust
1 cup warm water (105° to 115°)
1 ($^1/_4$-ounce) envelope active dry
  yeast
1 teaspoon honey
2 tablespoons extra-virgin olive oil,
  divided
3 cups unbleached all-purpose flour
1 teaspoon salt

In a large bowl, combine water, yeast, honey, and 1 tablespoon of olive oil, stirring to combine. Let sit until mixture is foamy, about 5 minutes.

Add $1^1/_2$ cups flour and the salt, mixing by hand until it is all incorporated and mixture is smooth. Continue adding flour, $^1/_4$ cup at a time, working dough after each addition, until it is smooth but still slightly sticky. You might not need all of the flour. Turn dough out onto a lightly floured surface and knead until dough is smooth but still slightly tacky, 3 to 5 minutes.

Oil a large mixing bowl with remaining olive oil. Place dough in the bowl, turning to coat with oil. Cover with plastic wrap and set in a warm place, free from drafts until doubled in size, about $1^1/_2$ hours.

After dough has risen, punch dough down, and on a floured surface roll dough out into desired size.

Pesto Sauce
$1^1/_2$ cups fresh basil leaves (packed)
$^1/_2$ teaspoon salt
$^1/_4$ teaspoon freshly ground black
  pepper
$^1/_4$ cup freshly grated Parmigiano-
  Reggiano
2 tablespoons pine nuts or walnuts,
  toasted
1 teaspoon minced garlic
$^1/_2$ cup extra-virgin olive oil

In bowl of a food processor, combine basil, salt, and pepper and process for a few seconds until basil is chopped. Add cheese, pine nuts, and garlic. While the processor is running, add oil in a thin, steady stream until a mostly smooth sauce is formed.

Transfer pesto to a bowl and set aside.

Pizza
1 (10-ounce) pizza crust
$^1/_4$ cup pesto sauce
$^3/_4$ cup chicken breast, cooked
  and diced
$^1/_4$ cup red onion, diced
6 grape tomatoes, halved
1 cup baby spinach, shredded
1 cup four-cheese blend, shredded
$^1/_4$ cup crumbled feta

Preheat oven to 450°.

Spread pesto on pizza crust and top with spinach. Place four-cheese blend on top of spinach, then top with remaining ingredients.

Bake pizza for approximately 15 to 20 minutes.

For Large Pizza
Use a 16-ounce crust and double ingredients.

" I think it's

important to have

a **heartfelt**

passion and a desire

to provide **wonderful**

service. "

Russell Logan
Executive Chef, Oak Crest
Parkville, Maryland

Formal training and experience: Russell received his formal culinary arts training from the Culinary Arts Institute at Johnson and Wales University in Providence, Rhode Island. He also was selected as the personal chef for the assistant commandant during his career with the United States Marine Corps.

"When I was young I remember helping my mother and father cook and can the vegetables we grew in the garden. Since then I always enjoyed working in the food service business. I think it's important to have a heartfelt passion and a desire to provide wonderful service. I want people to enjoy the fruits of my labor."

Out of the kitchen: "I try to spend as much time with my wife and kids as I possibly can." ☆

Maryland Crab Cakes

Serves 4

1 pound jumbo lump crabmeat
¼ cup breadcrumbs
½ cup mayonnaise
1 tablespoon dijon mustard
1 teaspoon lemon juice
1 egg, beaten
1 cup butter, melted

Pick over crabmeat and remove all shell pieces. Do not break up crabmeat any more than necessary. Drain any extra liquid.

Combine mayonnaise, mustard, lemon juice, and egg. Stir until smooth.

Add breadcrumbs to mayonnaise mixture. Mix until well blended.

Fold in crabmeat and gently mix, being careful not to break up lumps of crabmeat.

Portion crab mixture into ⅔-cup portions and form into patties.

Fried

Melt butter in a pan and gently place crabcakes in the pan and cook for 3 to 4 minutes per side.

Baked

Lightly grease baking dish with 2 tablespoons of melted butter. Gently place crabcakes in the baking dish so they are not touching. Drizzle remaining melted butter over crabcakes. Bake in a 400° oven for 15 to 20 minutes until golden brown.

Chef tip: For a little extra spice, add Old Bay™ or our Old Bay™ substitute recipe on page 13, to taste.

Beef, Veal, and Pork Meatloaf

Serves 4

Mirepoix Mixture:
¼ cup Spanish onion, diced
1½ tablespoons celery, diced
1½ tablespoons carrot, peeled &
    diced

Tomato Glaze:
4½ tablespoons ketchup
2 teaspoons brown sugar
2 teaspoons apple cider vinegar
½ tablespoon Worcestershire
    sauce
½ tablespoon steak sauce

Meatloaf:
1 pound ground beef
½ pound ground pork
½ pound ground veal
1 teaspoon garlic, chopped

½ cup mirepoix mixture
½ cup plain breadcrumbs
2 medium eggs, beaten
3 tablespoons Worcestershire
    sauce
3 tablespoons ketchup
2½ tablespoons mustard
2½ tablespoons steak sauce
¼ teaspoon steak seasoning

Place mirepoix mixture in a perforated pan and steam until tender, 8-10 minutes. Place mirepoix in food processor and process until mirepoix is finely ground.

Mix all ingredients for glaze. Heat slowly until sugar dissolves. Set aside.

Blend all meatloaf ingredients together and form meat mixture into loaves and place on parchment-lined baking sheet.

Bake in 350° oven for 45 to 55 minutes or until internal temperature reads 165°.

Spoon glaze over meatloaves after 30 minutes. Repeat every 10 minutes until meatloaves are done.

Chef tip: Mirepoix originated in France and is a traditional flavor base of many dishes. It can include, but isn't limited to, onion, carrot, and celery.

Crunchy Peach Cobbler

Serves 6

2 (16-ounce) cans cling peach slices
   in syrup
$\frac{1}{3}$ cup + 1 tablespoon granulated sugar, divided
1 tablespoon cornstarch
$\frac{1}{2}$ teaspoon vanilla
$\frac{1}{2}$ cup packed brown sugar
2 cups all-purpose flour, divided
$\frac{1}{3}$ cup uncooked rolled oats
$\frac{1}{4}$ cup butter, melted
$\frac{1}{2}$ teaspoon ground cinnamon
$\frac{1}{2}$ teaspoon salt
$\frac{1}{2}$ cup solid shortening
4 to 5 tablespoons cold water
Whipped topping, for serving

Drain peach slices, reserving $\frac{3}{4}$ cup syrup. Combine $\frac{1}{3}$ cup sugar and cornstarch in a small saucepan. Slowly add reserved peach liquid, stirring to make sauce smooth; add vanilla. Cook over low heat, stirring constantly, until thickened. Set aside.

Combine brown sugar, $\frac{1}{2}$ cup flour, oats, butter, and cinnamon in small bowl; stir until crumbly. Set aside.

Preheat oven to 350°. Combine remaining 1$\frac{1}{2}$ cups flour, 1 tablespoon sugar, and salt in a small bowl. Cut in shortening until mixture resembles coarse crumbs. Sprinkle water, 1 tablespoon at a time, over flour mixture and toss lightly until mixture holds together.

Shape into a ball. Roll out on floured surface to 10-inch square. Place in 8x8-inch baking dish. Press on bottom and about 1 inch up the sides. Layer peaches, sauce, and crumb topping over crust. Bake 45 minutes. Serve warm or at room temperature with whipped topping.

51

Girl Scout™ Peanut Butter Cream Pie

Serves 8

1 (8 ounce) package cream cheese,
  softened
¾ cup confectioners' sugar
½ cup peanut butter
2 tablespoons milk
1 cup crumbled Girl Scout™
  Peanut Butter Cookies
2 cups heavy cream, whipped
  until thick
1 (9-inch) graham cracker pie crust

Using a mixer with a whip attachment, beat confectioners' sugar and cream cheese until smooth. Add peanut butter, milk, and crumbled cookies to cream cheese mixture and beat well.

Fold whipped cream into peanut butter mixture; pour filling into prepared crust. Refrigerate pie at least 2 hours before cutting to serve.

Apple Cobbler with Streusel Topping

Serves 4

5 cups tart apples, peeled and sliced
³⁄₄ cup sugar
2 tablespoons all-purpose flour
¹⁄₂ teaspoon cinnamon
¹⁄₄ teaspoon salt
1 teaspoon vanilla extract
¹⁄₄ cup water
1 tablespoon butter, softened

Topping:
¹⁄₂ cup all-purpose flour, sifted
¹⁄₂ cup sugar
¹⁄₄ teaspoon salt
2 tablespoons butter, softened

In a medium bowl, mix together apples, sugar, flour, cinnamon, salt, vanilla, and water. Spoon apple mixture into a lightly buttered 9-inch square baking pan. Dot apples with 1 tablespoon butter.

Combine all topping ingredients and mix together until crumbs form. Sprinkle topping over apple mixture. Bake 35 to 40 minutes at 375° or until apples are tender. Serve warm with cream or ice cream.

Elegant Evening

Everyday cooking is quick, easy, and inexpensive by design. Then there are dishes that are a bit more complicated, take extra time to prepare, or use extraordinary ingredients—the very things that make them special.

The recipes in "Elegant Evening" are distinctive dishes we prepare on occasion in our restaurants. Discover succulent seafood, exotic soups, and sophisticated desserts in this section. Whether you cook them to celebrate an anniversary or simply to take a detour from daily life, these dishes let you explore a variety of flavorful, sumptuous tastes. ★

"You don't have to cook fancy or complicated masterpieces—just good food from fresh ingredients."

-Julia Child

"Cook with your senses. Recipes are just a starting point; it is up to the cook to give life to a dish."

-Jim Rondinelli, Linden Ponds

Mark Diller
Executive Chef, Ann's Choice
Warminster, Pennsylvania

Formal training and experience: Mark has been in the business for 25 years, getting his start working with his mother who ran all the kitchens in the local school district. He's covered every base, from short-order to fine dining.

"My philosophy is to use the very best ingredients to achieve the best end product possible. That's exactly what I try to do each day in the kitchens at Ann's Choice. I enjoy this business and I also really enjoy working with the people who live here and giving them what they want. When someone asks for something, I go out of my way to make it happen."

Out of the kitchen: "I am a die-hard Phillies fan. I also enjoy traveling and live music." ☆

" Ann's Choice has some of the area's best food critics. "

Mark F. Diller

Lobster and Asparagus Coquilles

Serves 4

$3\frac{1}{2}$ tablespoons butter, divided
1 shallot, finely chopped
1 pound lobster meat, diced (thawed and drained if frozen)
1 bunch cooked fresh asparagus, diced
$\frac{1}{4}$ teaspoon lemon juice
3 tablespoons all-purpose flour
2 cups hot milk
$\frac{1}{4}$ teaspoon nutmeg
1 cup grated Emmental cheese, divided
Salt and pepper
Pinch of ground cloves

Heat one teaspoon butter in saucepan. Add shallot and cook 1 minute over medium heat. Stir in lobster, asparagus, and lemon juice; cover and simmer 6 to 7 minutes over very low heat.

Heat remaining butter in second saucepan. Mix in flour and cook 2 minutes over low heat, stirring constantly. Add salt and pepper to taste and cook 6 to 7 minutes over low heat.

Pour in milk and season with nutmeg and cloves; blend well with a whisk. Season to taste and cook 6 to 7 minutes over low heat.

Transfer lobster and asparagus mixture to saucepan containing butter sauce. Mix in $\frac{1}{2}$ cup cheese and simmer 1 to 2 minutes.

Spoon mixture into scallop shells (or individual ramekins), top with remaining cheese, and broil until golden brown.

Serve immediately.

Zesty Shrimp in Phyllo

Serves 4

1 pound sautéed shrimp, small diced
¾ cup roasted garlic
1 roasted red pepper, minced
1 dash hot sauce
¾ teaspoon salt
¾ teaspoon white pepper
¼ cup peppercinis, minced
¾ cup bread crumbs
Phyllo pastry sheets
2 sticks butter for basting, melted

Preheat oven to 400°.

Brush each sheet of phyllo with melted butter. Keep unbuttered sheets covered with a moist cloth to prevent drying.

Combine remaining ingredients except shrimp in blender and blend well. Pour blended mixture into a large mixing bowl. Stir in diced shrimp; mix well and set aside.

Stack three pastry sheets together and cut in half. Place 1 tablespoon of filling in butter-basted, halved pastry sheets. Fold edges over the filling and seal pastry packets with a drop of water. Repeat until all filling is used.

Bake packets until golden brown, about 7 to 8 minutes.

Anjou Pear and Apple Salad with Balsamic Apple Cider Vinaigrette
Serves 6

SALAD

¹⁄₂ **pound pears, medium sliced**
¹⁄₂ **pound Granny Smith apples,
  sliced**
¹⁄₂ **pound dried cherries**
¹⁄₄ **cup lemon juice**
¹⁄₂ **pound variety mixed salad
  greens, chopped**
¹⁄₂ **pound feta cheese, crumbled**
¹⁄₂ **pound cooked rotini pasta**
2 tablespoons chopped parsley
Romaine lettuce

Stir lemon juice into 1 cup warm water. Toss apples and pears together. Let soak for 15 minutes in lemon mixture.

In mixing bowl, toss pears, apples, cherries, parsley, and pasta. Add salad greens and feta cheese, toss and mix lightly.

Ladle dressing over salad, toss and mix lightly so that the pasta noodles do not break up. Line six chilled plates with crisp romaine leaves, then divide salad among plates.

Garnish top of salads with additional slices apple and sprinkle with dried cherries. Serve with warm rolls or bread.

DRESSING
Yields about 2 cups

¹⁄₄ **cup apple cider**
¹⁄₂ **cup balsamic vinegar**
1 cup olive oil
¹⁄₂ **cup honey**
¹⁄₂ **teaspoon cinnamon**
¹⁄₂ **teaspoon salt**
1 teaspoon black pepper
1 tablespoon granulated garlic

In a mixing bowl combine all ingredients except olive oil. Mix well with a wire whisk. Slowly drizzle in olive oil to emulsify dressing.

Let stand 5 minutes. Remix before pouring over salad.

Sherried Oyster and Brie Soup

Serves 4

1 quart select oysters with liquor
2 tablespoons butter
1 pound fresh mushrooms, thinly sliced
½ cup shallots, minced
2 tablespoons fresh lemon juice
2 tablespoons all-purpose flour
3 cups beef broth
1 cup cream sherry, reduced to ½ cup*
4 ounces brie cheese, rind trimmed
1 cup milk
1 cup heavy cream
Salt and pepper to taste
Chives for garnish

Drain oysters and reserve liquor, set aside. Melt butter in large saucepan over medium-high heat. When butter is melted, stir in mushrooms, shallots, and lemon juice; cook and stir 2 minutes. Sprinkle with flour; cook and stir 1 minute more. Add broth and reduced sherry. Bring to a boil; reduce heat and simmer 20 minutes.

Add brie and stir to melt. Stir in reserved oyster liquor, milk, and cream; season with salt and pepper. Heat until very hot. Do not boil. Remove from heat and add oysters. Cover and let stand until oysters are just plumped. Garnish with fresh chives.

*To reduce, simmer over medium heat until slightly thickened and reduced to desired amount.

Shrimp Bisque

Serves 6

½ cup carrot, diced
½ cup celery, diced
⅔ cup onion, minced
3½ teaspoons margarine
1¼ teaspoons garlic, peeled, minced
2 bay leaves
1 teaspoon Old Bay™
1¾ teaspoons paprika
3½ teaspoons tomato paste
1½ cups water
3½ teaspoons shrimp base (no MSG)
1¾ cups milk
2½ tablespoons all-purpose flour

3½ teaspoons margarine
¼ pound raw shrimp, peeled and diced
4 tablespoons cooking sherry
White pepper
Hot sauce to taste

Sauté onion, garlic, celery, and carrot in pot with 3½ teaspoons margarine. Add bay leaves, Old Bay™, tomato paste, and paprika. Continue cooking for a few minutes.

Add water and shrimp base and simmer for 1 hour. Strain bisque through a fine strainer and return to a simmer. Add milk.

Meanwhile, sauté shrimp and set aside.

In a small saucepan, melt 3½ teaspoons margarine and stir in flour to make roux. Stir roux into bisque to thicken slightly.

Cook uncovered for 30 minutes over low heat, allowing bisque to simmer. Add shrimp and stir in. Stir in the sherry slowly. Add white pepper and hot sauce to taste.

Chef tip: Old Bay™ is a regional seasoning and may be hard to find away from the Chesapeake region, use our Old Bay™ substitute recipe on page 13.

Hubbard Squash Soup

Serves 4

$\frac{1}{4}$ cup celery, diced
$\frac{1}{4}$ cup onion, diced
$\frac{1}{4}$ cup carrots, diced
$1\frac{1}{4}$ teaspoons nutmeg
$1\frac{1}{4}$ teaspoons cinnamon
$\frac{1}{4}$ tablespoon ground ginger
$\frac{1}{3}$ cup butter
$\frac{1}{2}$ cup sifted flour
$1\frac{1}{2}$ cups chicken stock
$\frac{1}{3}$ cup heavy cream
1 ($2\frac{1}{2}$ pound) package whipped hubbard squash
Salt and pepper to taste

Sauté celery, onion, and carrot together with butter, nutmeg, cinnamon, and ground ginger. Cook for about 5 minutes.

Add flour to mix and combine to make roux. Cook for another 10 to 15 minutes on low to medium heat, stirring constantly.

Add chicken stock and bring to boil. Add squash, stirring constantly. Let boil for at least 20 minutes on low flame. Add salt and pepper to taste. Stir in cream immediately before serving.

{ chef profile }

Samuel Soto
Executive Chef, Greenspring
Springfield, Virginia

Formal training and experience: Samuel began developing his culinary skills while enlisted in the U.S. Air Force and later while attending the Culinary Institute of America. Before joining Greenspring he worked for Marriot Hotels.

"I always make sure to take time and walk around the tables in the restaurants while people are eating because I enjoy the honest, open, and constructive interactions I get. Patience, organization, and being a good listener are all qualities I believe a good chef should possess."

Out of the kitchen: "I enjoy playing golf, racquetball, riding my bike, and flying kites." ✫

> " I **always** make sure to take time and **walk around** the tables in the restaurants. "

Spring Vegetables with Lemon and Shallots

Serves 6

3 pounds fresh fava beans, shelled
2 tablespoons olive oil, divided
1 tablespoon unsalted butter, divided
4 shallots, finely sliced
1 pound sugar snap peas, trimmed
1 pound asparagus, trimmed and cut diagonally
    into ½-inch slices
2 (3-inch) strips lemon zest, julienned
2 teaspoons fresh lemon juice
Salt and pepper to taste

To prepare fava beans, blanch for 1 minute, then cool and remove outer skins. 1 pound frozen Fordhook lima beans may be substituted for fava beans and should be prepared in the same manner and set aside.

In a large skillet, heat 1 tablespoon oil and ½ tablespoon butter over moderately high heat until foam subsides. Sauté shallots, stirring until tender, about 2 minutes.

With a slotted spoon transfer shallots to a bowl. In the fat remaining in skillet, sauté snap peas with salt to taste, stirring occasionally until crisp yet tender. Add shallots.

In skillet, heat remaining oil and butter over moderately high heat until foam subsides. Sauté asparagus with salt to taste, stirring occasionally, until crisp yet tender. Add fava or lima beans and sauté, stirring occasionally, about 2 minutes.

Add zest, lemon juice, snap peas, shallots, and salt and pepper to taste and sauté until just heated through.

Wonton Purses

Serves 20

2 tablespoons button mushrooms,
    chopped
$\frac{1}{2}$ pound ground pork
$\frac{1}{4}$ cup frozen spinach, thawed
    and drained
$2\frac{1}{4}$ teaspoons sherry
1 teaspoon soy sauce
$\frac{1}{2}$ teaspoon grated ginger
$\frac{1}{2}$ tablespoon Cumberland sauce
$\frac{1}{4}$ teaspoon dry mustard
$\frac{1}{4}$ teaspoon wasabi powder
Wonton wrappers (usually found in
    the produce section near the tofu)
Cornstarch to seal purses

Sauté pork until cooked. Add mushrooms and ginger and blend well.

Add remaining ingredients and blend well.

Spoon small amount of filling into wonton wrapper and fold like a purse using water and cornstarch mixture to seal.

Place purses in Chinese bamboo steamer in wok over rapidly boiling water. Steam until dough is firm and has opaque, milky color, about 5 minutes.

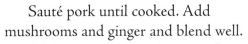 Chef tip: Cumberland sauce is a fruit based sauce commonly paired with pork. Ingredients may include red currants, wine, mustard, pepper, vinegar, and ginger.

Crab Imperial

Serves 10

1 medium green pepper, finely chopped
2 pimentos, finely chopped
1 tablespoon English mustard
Salt to taste
¼ teaspoon white pepper
2 eggs, beaten
1 cup mayonnaise
3 pounds crabmeat (back fin or lump)
1 teaspoon paprika or seafood seasoning
¼ cup breadcrumbs
¼ cup sherry wine
Lemon wedges for garnish

In a large mixing bowl combine the first 7 ingredients and mix well.

Add sherry and crabmeat and mix well, taking care not to break up crab.

Place about ½ cup of mixture into a baking dish (clam shell or gratin dish). Top lightly with paprika or seafood seasoning and breadcrumbs.

Place individual dishes on a baking sheet and bake at 350° for 15 minutes or until an internal temperature of 145.°

Serve immediately with assorted crackers and garnish with lemon wedges.

Honey Dijon Salmon

Serves 4

4 salmon steaks
$\frac{1}{2}$ cup honey
2 tablespoons dijon mustard
$1\frac{1}{2}$ tablespoons melted butter
   or margarine
2 teaspoons Worcestershire sauce
1 tablespoon cornstarch
$\frac{1}{8}$ teaspoon white pepper
1 pound fresh asparagus
$\frac{1}{3}$ cup chopped walnuts

   Preheat oven to 450°. Prepare 4 (12x18-inch) sheets of aluminum foil and set aside.

   Blend honey, mustard, butter, Worcestershire sauce, cornstarch, and pepper. Set aside.

   Center $\frac{1}{4}$ of asparagus on each sheet of foil. Top with salmon steaks.

   Drizzle with $\frac{1}{4}$ of honey-mustard sauce and top with $\frac{1}{4}$ of walnuts.

   Bring up the sides of the foil to meet in the middle. Double-fold the top and ends to seal packet, leaving a pocket of air for heat circulation inside. Repeat to make three other packets.

   Place packets on a baking sheet and bake 17 to 23 minutes. Carefully pierce packets allowing steam to release before opening.

Chicken Woodland

Serves 4

4 boneless, skinless chicken breasts
Flour (for dredging)
2 eggs, beaten
1 cup mushrooms, sliced
1 shallot, minced
½ cup olive oil
1 cup light cream
1 teaspoon fresh chopped parsley
Salt & pepper to taste

Pound chicken breasts lightly. Heat oil in skillet until hot (not smoking). Dip chicken into flour and then into beaten eggs. Sauté in oil until lightly browned on both sides. Place chicken in an ovenproof dish and bake at 350° for 15 to 20 minutes or until fully cooked.

Drain excess oil from browning pan and add shallots and mushrooms. Sauté until all liquid from mushrooms has evaporated. Add cream and simmer until slightly thickened.

Ladle sauce over chicken and sprinkle with chopped parsley to serve.

Orange Roughy Tarragon

Serves 4

4 (5-ounce) orange roughy fillets, thawed
Nonstick cooking spray
2 lemons, 1 halved and 1 sliced
$2\frac{1}{2}$ tablespoons butter
2 tablespoons fresh tarragon, finely chopped
$\frac{1}{8}$ teaspoon white pepper
$\frac{2}{3}$ cup chardonnay
2 teaspoons paprika

Place fish in sprayed, 9 x 13-inch baking pan.

Squeeze juice from halved lemon into container. Combine with butter, wine, and pepper. Brush butter blend on fish and sprinkle with paprika.

Cook fish at 350° until internal temperature reaches 145°, about 10 to 12 minutes. Make twists from sliced lemon and place on each piece of fish as garnish. Serve immediately.

Braised Lamb Shank with Garlic Infused Lamb Reduction

Serves 4

Lamb Shanks

4 lamb shanks
Kosher salt and pepper
1½ tablespoons olive oil
1 onion, peeled and diced into ¼ inch pieces
1 carrot, peeled and diced into ¼ inch pieces
1 stalk celery, diced into ¼ inch pieces
1 head garlic, peeled and minced
1 cup red wine
2 quarts lamb stock or low sodium beef broth

Preheat oven to 275°. Season lamb shanks with salt and pepper. Heat oil in large pot (should be deep enough to hold lamb shanks and cooking liquid) and brown meat on all sides and remove from pot. Add onion, carrot, celery, and garlic to the pot and sweat until onions are translucent and just begin to brown.

Remove pan from heat and add red wine to deglaze (being sure to scrape the bottom of the pan to release all of the caramelized bits and pieces of meat and vegetables). Place lamb back into pot and add stock. Cover with a lid and place in oven (add liquid if necessary). Cook for 4 to 6 hours or until meat is very tender. Remove from oven and let rest in cooking liquid.

Garlic-Infused Lamb Reduction

1 onion, peeled and chopped coarsely
1 carrot, peeled and chopped coarsely
2 stalks celery, peeled and chopped coarsely
3 tablespoons bacon fat or olive oil
2 cups red wine
1 quart braising liquid, skimmed to remove fat

In hot pan, add bacon fat or olive oil. Add and sweat onion, carrot, celery, and garlic. When onions are translucent and just start to brown, remove pan from heat and add red wine to deglaze. Add the braising liquid and cook over medium heat until liquid has reduced to roughly one cup. Strain if desired and keep warm until serving time.

Spoon warm sauce over lamb shanks to serve.

Jason Fernandi
Executive Chef, Cedar Crest
Pompton Plains, New Jersey

Formal training and experience: After graduating from the Academy of Culinary Arts in Mays Landing, New Jersey, Jason enjoyed working in the kitchens of a variety of popular Manhattan restaurants including Gramercy Tavern, Gotham Bar and Grill, Union Pacific Café, and Café Boulud.

"I inherited my love of cooking from my mother and grandmother. It wasn't until college, however, that I decided to pursue it as a career. At Cedar Crest, I spend a lot of my time coming up with new dishes and recipes. I think it is important to use only the freshest foods and not to cut corners when it comes to quality."

Out of the kitchen: "Believe it or not I love cooking at home. I cook every night when I get home. I also enjoy painting and sketching, as well as playing the jazz guitar." ☆

" I refuse to cut corners when it comes to quality. "

Soft Shell Crabs with Fingerling Potatoes

Serves 4

12 fingerling potatoes, washed
1 cup fresh fava beans
1 pound broccoli rabe, stalks removed
12 medium soft shell crabs
Sea salt and fresh white pepper
6 tablespoons grapeseed oil (may substitute canola)
2 tablespoons olive oil
2 cloves garlic, thinly sliced
10 tablespoons unsalted butter, divided
½ cup heavy cream
3 tablespoons fresh lemon juice
Chives, chopped for garnish

For the vegetables

Cook potatoes over high heat in a pot of boiling salted water for about 10 to 15 minutes or until tender. Remove from heat and let stand in cooking liquid.

Cook fava beans in salted water until tender, about 3 minutes. Drain beans and immediately immerse them in ice water. Peel the skins.

Cook broccoli rabe in salted boiling water for 2 to 3 minutes or until tender but still a vibrant green color. Drain and keep warm.

For the sauce

Add 8 tablespoons of butter to a sauté pan over medium-high heat and melt. Continue to cook until butter begins to brown. Add lemon juice and cream. Reduce cream by half or until thick enough to coat the back of a spoon. Season with salt and pepper and reserve.

For the crabs

Preheat oven to 450°. Season crabs with salt and pepper. Divide grapeseed oil between two 10 to 12-inch sauté pans and place on heat. When oil is very hot, but not yet smoking, add crabs, shell side down, and sauté until crisp, about 3 to 4 minutes. Turn crabs and place pans in oven for 4 to 5 minutes.

While crabs are cooking, cut potatoes into ¼-inch thick rounds and add them to a saucepan with a bit of the cooking liquid. Add fava beans and 2 tablespoons of butter and simmer. In a sauté pan heat 2 tablespoons of olive oil and add garlic. When garlic just begins to brown, add broccoli rabe and sauté until heated through, season if necessary.

In the center of four warmed dinner plates, spoon equal amounts of potatoes and fava beans. Place broccoli rabe on top and then 3 crabs. Spoon butter sauce over crabs and vegetables. Scatter with chives.

Seafood Turnovers with Lobster Sauce

Serves 10

1¼ pounds shrimp, diced
   and sautéd
1 pound Maine lobster meat,
   diced
1 pound Chiliean crabmeat
2 small carrots, diced
1 small onion, diced
¼ bunch celery, diced
8 cups hot water
6 tablespoons lobster base
1 dash hot sauce
1 tablespoon salt
½ tablespoon white pepper
½ pound butter
¾ cup all-purpose flour
2 pounds puff pastry dough for
   10 (3-inch) turnovers
1 egg, beaten

   Prepare lobster stock by stirring lobseter base into hot water. Set aside.

   In a heavy bottom pot, sauté vegetables in butter until tender.

   Add flour and cook for 5 minutes, slowly adding hot lobster stock, stirring often to avoid lumps. Allow to cool.

   Fold in seafood and wrap in puff pastry. Cut into 3-inch squares.

   Brush with egg and bake for 15 minutes at 350°.

Lobster Cognac Sauce

1 cup brandy
1 tablespoon lobster sauce
Pinch cayenne pepper
4 cups heavy cream

   In medium saucepan, combine brandy, lobster base, and cayenne. reduce to about one tablespoon.

   Add heavy cream and reduce until thick enough to coat a spoon.

Crème Brulée

Serves 5

4 egg yolks, beaten
1¹⁄₂ tablespoons brown sugar
1¹⁄₂ tablespoons white sugar
1¹⁄₈ cups heavy cream
¹⁄₄ tablespoon vanilla or vanilla
beans (split)
Pinch of salt

Combine yolks, salt, and sugars. Blend lightly to avoid air bubbles. Scald cream with vanilla.

Temper yolks and sugar with the cream before mixing entire amount.

Preheat oven to 300°.

Place 5 ramekins in a baking dish and fill each with custard mixture.

To prepare water bath, pour hot water into baking dish, about half way up the sides of the ramekins. Carefully place baking pan in center of oven and cook for 20 to 30 minutes until set.

Spread brown sugar evenly on baking sheet. Bake for 20 minutes, remove and cool. Place sugar in food processor, or use mortar and pestal to grind sugar until very fine. Sprinkle over baked custard and brown under broiler.

Chef tip: Historically, a pinch was defined as the amount that can be held between the thumb and forefinger.

Vanilla Bean Panna Cotta

Serves 4

1¾ teaspoons unflavored gelatin
2 cups heavy cream
6 tablespoons granulated sugar,
  divided
2 vanilla beans (or one table
  spoon vanilla extract)
¼ cup water
1 pint raspberries
Fresh mint sprigs for garnish

In a saucepan, combine cream and 2 tablespoons of sugar.

Split vanilla bean and scrape seeds. Add both seeds and pods to saucepan. Bring cream mixture to a boil and remove from heat. Allow mixture to steep for five minutes and return to the heat. Bring to a boil once again and remove from heat.

Add two more tablespoons of sugar and gelatin. Stir until gelatin has completely dissolved. Strain, then and cool mixture by pouring cream in a large bowl and then placing that bowl inside a larger bowl filled with ice.

Stir mixture until it is just cool to the touch. Pour mixture into ramekins and refrigerate for 2 to 3 hours, or until completely set.

For the compote

In a pan, combine water with 2 tablespoons of sugar. Heat gently over low heat until sugar has dissolved completely. Add fresh raspberries and heat until berries are slightly softened.

To assemble

Place bottom of each ramekin into warm water for 15 to 20 seconds. Invert ramekin onto a plate and tap firmly on bottom of ramekin until Panna Cotta releases. Spoon compote around base of Panna Cotta and top with a sprig of fresh mint.

Bananas Foster

Serves 4

1 stick (½ cup) unsalted butter
½ cup light brown sugar
4 ripe bananas, peeled and sliced
½ cup dark rum
½ teaspoon cinnamon
4 scoops vanilla ice cream

Melt butter in a skillet, add brown sugar, and heat mixture, stirring until sugar is caramelized. Add bananas and sauté three or four minutes, until warm. Sprinkle cinnamon over bananas.

Pour rum over bananas and flambé, continue cooking and baste bananas with the sauce until the flame burns out.

Divide ice cream equally into four dessert dishes and top each portion with banana and sauce mixture.

Chef tip: Ignite dish with a long match (such as fireplace matches or a long barbecue lighter). Always ignite the fumes at the edge of the pan and not the liquid itself.

Chefs' Picks

Even occasional cooks have a favorite recipe. It's your signature dish your friends request when they come for dinner and your family expects on special occasions.

Here are the recipes we hold near and dear to our hearts. They conjure up wonderful memories of family gatherings, favorite vacation spots, and special moments in our lives. Most of these personal favorites have only been served on special occasions at Erickson communities. We're excited to be able to share them with you now. ★

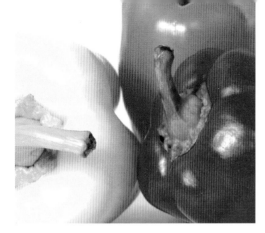  

"The most indispensable ingredient of all good home cooking: love, for those you are cooking for."

-Sophia Loren

"Cooking for yourself can be a great way to experiment. Veer off the beaten path. Just always make sure to do your test runs before a big event, like a holiday or Saturday night dinner."

-Mark Diller, Ann's Choice

Chef Vance Klein's Tomato Bisque

Serves 4 to 5

4 ripe tomatoes, diced
½ cup Spanish onions, diced
4 large cloves garlic
2 tablespoons olive oil
⅛ cup olive oil
⅔ cups parmesan cheese
2 cups marinara sauce
½ cup chicken broth
¼ cup sherry wine
2 cups heavy cream
1 cup whole milk
2 tablespoons fresh basil, chopped
2 tablespoons all-purpose flour
Salt and pepper to taste

Place garlic cloves and olive oil in an aluminum foil pouch and roast in oven for 25 minutes at 325°.

In a soup pot, sauté onion in 2 tablespoons olive oil until golden brown; add diced tomatoes and roasted garlic, including olive oil from the pouch.

Cook 3 minutes, sprinkle in flour and continue to stir for 1 to 2 minutes. Add sherry wine, marinara sauce, and chicken broth. Add salt and pepper to taste.

Bring to a simmer and cook for 3 minutes. Add heavy cream and milk. Continue to cook for 5 more minutes, then slowly sprinkle in parmesan cheese while whisking.

Remove soup from heat, and purée until smooth with a hand blender.

Stir in fresh basil before serving.

Chef Terry Shuster's Bacon, Lettuce, and Tomato Soup

Serves 6

1 (12-ounce) package bacon, diced
6 tablespoons bacon fat
¼ cup butter
½ cup onion, finely diced
6 tablespoons al-purpose flour
4 cups hot water (boiling)
¼ cup tomatoes, diced
2 tablespoons tomato paste
2 tablespoons chicken base
2 tablespoons Worchestershire sauce
1 head iceberg lettuce, julienned
Salt & pepper to taste

Cook bacon in heavy pot until crisp. Remove with a slotted spoon, drain and set aside. Pour off drippings and reserve. Add onion to pan and cook until soft. Add butter adn 6 tablespoons of reserved bacon fat back to pot.

Stir in flour and reduce heat. Cook 10 minutes, then slowly pour in boiling water, stirring to avoid lumps. Add chicken base, tomato paste, and diced tomatoes and bring to a boil. Stir in bacon bits and seasonings. Simmer 30 minutes.

Sauté julienned lettuce in small amount of bacon fat. Add to soup cups and pour hot soup over lettuce.

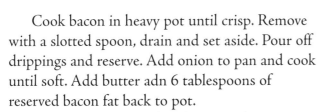

Chef tip: This soup goes great with grilled cheese sandwiches!

Jim Rondinelli
Chef de Cuisine, Linden Ponds
Hingham, Massachusetts

Formal training and experience: Jim began his career by traveling throughout New England as an apprentice with chefs from Copenhagen and France. He later reopened a local Boston landmark, The Cranebrook Tea Room, which received one of Boston's 1998 Zagat Guide Top 40 Restaurant awards.

"Because of my Italian heritage and closeness to my grandmother, somehow, I feel connected to their philosophy and affinity to the Old World. I believe in cooking with my senses and not relying so heavily on recipes. I think it's important to always keep in mind that a recipe alone has no personality until it is given life by the cook. So cook with your instincts, transcend technique, and be creative."

Out of the kitchen: "I enjoy traveling, golfing, reading, writing about cuisine, and raising my English cocker spaniels." ☆

" I believe in cooking with my **senses** and not relying so heavily on recipes. "

Jim Rondinelli

Chef Ron Colasanti's White Bean Soup With Escarole, Sweet Potatoes, and Sausage

Serves 6 to 8

1 cup dried white cannellini beans
½ cup dry, white table wine (optional)
4 cups low-sodium chicken broth
⅓ cup Spanish onion, medium dice
½ teaspoon garlic, minced
½ cup crushed tomatoes
2 large sweet potatoes, peeled and cut into
    ¼-inch cubes
⅓ cup carrot, medium dice
1 pound sweet Italian sausage, cooked and
    cut into ¼-inch pieces
1 head escarole lettuce, washed and cut
    into 1-inch pieces
2 bay leaves
Salt and pepper (to taste)
Parmesan cheese

Place white beans in a quart of cold water and refrigerate uncovered overnight.

The next day, drain and rinse beans and place them in a large stock pot with white wine, chicken broth, water, onion, garlic, and crushed tomatoes. Bring to a boil, lower heat, and allow to simmer uncovered until beans are almost cooked through, about 20 to 25 minutes.

Add sweet potatoes and carrot. Cooking until beans are soft, yet firm, and sweet potatoes are tender, about another 20 minutes.

Remove from heat. Carefully ladle about 2½ cups of broth and the bean-sweet potato mixture into a blender. Purée until smooth.

Add blended mixture back into the stock pot along with sausage, escarole, and bay leaves. Add salt and fresh ground black pepper to taste. Using a spoon, mix soup to incorporate the purée. Heat again on low for another 10 to 15 minutes.

Remove bay leaves. Serve warm drizzled with olive oil.

Pass parmesan cheese separately.

Chef Mark Diller's Chicken in Lemon Sauce

Serves 6

¼ cup butter
6 boneless chicken breast
¼ cup dry white wine
½ teaspoon grated lemon zest
2 tablespoon fresh lemon juice
1 cup heavy cream
1 cup fresh sliced mushrooms
⅓ cup parmesan cheese
Dash salt & white pepper
All-purpose flour for dredging

Melt butter in large skillet over medium heat; lightly dredge chicken in flour and sauté both sides 3 to 4 minutes; until cooked and tender. Remove chicken from skillet and set aside.

Add mushrooms to pan and cook 1 minute; add wine, lemon zest, and lemon juice; cook additional minute; add salt and pepper.

Gradually pour in cream, stirring constantly until hot; do not boil.

Add chicken to sauce; toss lightly; remove chicken to platter topping with remaining sauce.

Sprinkle with parmesan cheese.

Serve immediately.

Chef Wayne Knowles' Butterflied Leg of Lamb

Serves 8-10

Marinade:
2 cups fresh lemon juice
6 cups olive oil
2 bunches fresh parsley,
  chopped
6 bay leaves, crumbled
6 large white onions,
  thinly sliced
6 cloves garlic, crushed
⅓ cup dried oregano leaves
1 bunch fresh mint,
  chopped
2 tablespoons cracked
pepper

Lamb:
1 boneless leg of lamb
honey for rubbing

Combine all marinade ingredients; blend well and set aside.

Using boneless leg of lamb, butterfly large muscles so that meat is approximately same thickness throughout. Trim and discard excess fat.

Liberally rub meat on both sides with honey and place in marinade. Allow to marinate 12 to 48 hours. Remove from marinade, pat dry and grill to desired doneness. Internal temperature should be at least 145° Allow meat to rest before slicing.

Chef tip: If you don't have fresh mint, use mint tea from an herbal tea bag, parsley, or basil.

" My mom

taught me to

cook and let me

help her. "

Wayne Knowles

Wayne Knowles
Corporate Executive Chef

Formal training and experience: After graduating from the Culinary Institute of America at Hyde Park in New York, Wayne worked as a chef for Hyatt Hotels and helped open the Baltimore Hyatt Regency and the Grand Cypress in Florida. He also worked for Disney and had his own restaurant.

"My mother and my grandmothers were fabulous cooks. I guess that's part of the reason I started cooking at a young age. I liked playing around in the kitchen so my Mom taught me to cook and let me help her. By high school, I was really into sports. But when I'd come home complaining of hunger, my Mom would tell me to cook something for myself. It would look so good, she'd say, 'Why don't you just cook something for all of us.' And I would."

Out of the kitchen: "I really enjoy gardening and landscaping. But my passion is life on the water—salt water fishing and boating. I also like historical research. One subject in particular I'm interested in is the John W. Brown, a World War II liberty ship here in Baltimore that is on theNational Register of Historical Places."

Chef Wayne Knowles' Chicken and Pasta Chardonnay

Serves 4

1 (1½-pound) fresh, whole chicken

3 quarts water

3 bay leaves

½ teaspoon whole black pepper corns

¼ teaspoon dried thyme leaf

¼ cup heavy cream

1 tablespoon cornstarch

¼ cup chardonnay wine

¼ yellow squash, julienne

¼ cup fresh carrots, julienne

Pencil-thin asparagus, cut into 2-inch pieces (about ¼ cup)

2 tablespoons scallions, chopped

¼ cup fresh spinach, chopped

¼ cup penne pasta

2 tablespoons fresh chopped basil

2 tablespoons shredded parmesan cheese

Wash chicken and place into a 1-gallon pot. Add bay leaves, peppercorns, thyme, and water.

Bring water to a boil and reduce heat. Simmer for 30 to 45 minutes. Do not boil! Skim away foam that rises to the top of stock.

After the chicken has cooked enough to make a rich stock, strain and pour into another pot. Place chicken on a sheet tray or platter to cool.

Return chicken stock to heat and bring to a boil. Allow chicken stock to boil and reduce for 15 to 20 minutes (this will intensify the flavor).

Cook pasta al dente. After chicken has cooled, pick all meat from bones. Carefully remove peppercorns and bay leaves from chicken meat. Discard bones. Cut chicken into bite-size pieces. Place carrots into chicken stock and cook for 4 minutes (they require a longer cooking time than the other vegetables). Mix wine with the cornstarch and stir until smooth. Slowly pour this into chicken stock and vegetable mixture while stirring. Stir gently until stock turns clear.

After 4 minutes add squash and asparagus. After 2 minutes add chicken meat, pasta, spinach, scallions, and heavy cream to mixture. Allow mixture to simmer for 2 to 3 minutes. Serve in soup plates or platter topped with chopped basil and shredded cheese.

Chef Mohammad Bayan's
Leg of Lamb with Yogurt

Serves 8 to 10

1 leg of lamb
1½ cup plain yogurt
2 tablespoons tomato paste
6 garlic cloves, crushed
1 teaspoon black pepper
1 teaspoon cardamom
1 teaspoon cinnamon
1 teaspoon cumin
1 teaspoon saffron
1 teaspoon salt
9 tablespoons corn oil
3 tablespoons mayonnaise

Rinse meat and pat dry. Make several cuts across the width of the leg. Put in a baking pan. Mix remaining ingredients together and spread half of mixture over meat.

Cover with foil and cook at 350° until meat reaches an internal temperature of 130° (approximately 1 ½ hours).

This should cook meat to medium-rare. (If you prefer your meat more well-done, leave it in the oven longer.)

After removing from the oven, lightly cover meat with the remaining mixture and allow to sit 10 to 15 minutes before slicing.

Chef tip: Use 2 teaspoons of Italian seasoning or 2 teaspoons of lemon zest or lemon juice as an alternative to 1 teaspoon of salt.

Chef James Little Jr.'s Seafood Macaroni & Cheese

Serves 8

1 pound medium-sized pasta shells
½ cup sharp cheese, cubed
½ cup monterey jack cheese, cubed
½ cup mozzarella cheese, cubed
½ cup cheddar cheese, cubed
1 cup Velveeta™
3 cups whole milk
1½ tablespoons season-all
2 tablespoons seafood seasoning
1 bay leaf
½ teaspoon garlic salt
½ teaspoon onion powder
1 cup small shrimp
½ cup bay scallops
1 cup back fin crabmeat

Cook pasta al dente; drain and set aside.

In a large sauce pan, add milk, bay leaf, Velveeta™, and all dry spices. Stir frequently over medium-low heat until blended.

Blanch all seafood until firm.

In large mixing bowl, combine reserved pasta, seafood, and cheeses. Spoon mixture into buttered casserole dish.

Pour seasoned Velveeta™ sauce over contents of casserole dish. Bake in a 325° oven between 35 and 45 minutes.

Lightly dust with additional seafood seasoning and serve.

Chef Mark Badin's Beef Goulash with Spaetzle

Serves 6-8

Beef Goulash

2 tablespoons olive oil or bacon fat
4 cups thinly sliced onions
1 tablespoon sugar
3 garlic cloves, minced
1 tablespoon ground caraway seed
1½ tablespoons sweet paprika
1 teaspoon spicy paprika
1 tablespoon marjoram dry ground
1 teaspoon thyme leaves
2 bay leaves
3 tablespoons tomato paste
4 cups chicken stock
2½ pounds beef shank, cut into
2-inch julienne strips
1 teaspoon kosher salt
¼ teaspoon black pepper
2 tomatoes, chopped (or 6-ounce
can chopped tomatoes)
2 tablespoons red wine vinegar
Sour cream for garnish

In a large sauté pan, sauté onions in olive oil or bacon fat. Add sugar and sauté until it caramelizes. Add garlic and caraway seed. Sauté 1 minute. Add all remaining herbs and spices, except salt and pepper, and sauté 1 minute until fragrant. Add tomato paste, cook for 2 minutes.

While the pan is still hot, deglaze it with vinegar and chicken stock. It will flash and steam a little and start to simmer. Carefully scrape bottom of pan to loosen any browned bits.

Add beef shank, salt, and pepper and bring to a boil, lower to a simmer, and cook until very tender, approximately 1½ hours, stirring occasionally.

Garnish with sour cream. (Coachman's version is served with sunny side up eggs on top.)

Spaetzle

2 eggs
2 tablespoons bacon fat or
vegetable oil
½ cup water
½ cup milk
2½ cups all-purpose flour
2½ teaspoons salt
¼ teaspoon baking powder
1 teaspoon nutmeg

Mix all ingredients well except bacon fat or oil; batter should have consistency of sticky waffle batter.

In a large stock pot, bring water on a rolling boil.

Pour batter through a spaetzle maker, potato ricer, or sieve into the boiling water. When spaetzle floats to the top of pot, remove and drain, reserving water.

Let water return to a rolling boil before continuing with remaining batter. When all the spaetzle has been boiled you may serve it as is or add "clothes" by sautéing in vegetable oil or bacon fat.

{ chef profile }

" It is just as

important to

manage your staff

well as it is to know

where the

ingredients go. **"**

Mark Badin
Executive Chef, Charlestown
Catonsville, Maryland

Formal training and experience: Over the course of 18 years Mark worked his way up from dishwasher through all of the culinary positions in the Disney Culinary Apprenticeship. He also attended the California Culinary Academy in San Francisco and the Culinary Institute of America in Napa Valley.

"I enjoy the friendly atmosphere at Charlestown, as well as the fact that I get the chance to build long-term relationships with the people who live here. I believe that to be a chef, it is just as important to manage your staff well as it is to know where the ingredients go and when."

Out of the kitchen: "I like to read and spend time with my three children." ☆

Chef Wayne Knowles' Dried Fruit Cream Scones

Serves 10

Scones:
2 cups all-purpose flour
1 tablespoon baking powder
½ teaspoon salt
¼ cup sugar
½ cup chopped dried fruit (apricots, prunes, or figs)
¼ cup golden raisins
1¼ cups heavy cream

Glaze:
3 tablespoons butter, melted
2 tablespoons sugar

Preheat oven to 425°. Combine flour, baking powder, salt, and sugar in a bowl, stirring with a fork to mix well. Add dried fruit and raisins.

Still using a fork, stir in cream and mix until the dough holds together but is still quite sticky. Lightly flour a board and transfer the dough to it. Knead dough 8 or 9 minutes. Pat into a circle about 10 inches round. Transfer dough to an ungreased baking sheet.

For the glaze
Brush butter over top and side of dough and sprinkle the sugar on top. Cut circle into 12 wedges and place each piece on the baking sheet allowing about an inch between pieces. Bake for about 15 minutes, or until golden brown.

Chef tip: Combine equal amounts of whole wheat and all-purpose flour o add extra fiber to a dish.

Behind the Scenes: Labor of Love

All great homemade dishes are a labor of love. If you start with the right ingredients, take the time to prepare, and pour your heart and soul into them you almost can't go wrong. The same can be said for the making of this cookbook. Our passion for food and cooking inspired us to go about creating this collection of recipes in a "home-made" fashion. We're just a bunch of chefs from all over the country who came together to exchange our ideas, prepare our dishes, and have them photographed for this cookbook.

There's a saying that goes, "Do what you love and you'll never work a day in your life." It couldn't be more true for each of us. Throughout the making of this book we laughed, joked, shared stories, exchanged cooking tips, and in the end created a cookbook that simply reflects the foods we love. We hope you'll love them too! So go ahead and get cooking … and most importantly have fun!

"

„

Notes

"

„

Index

Index

Index